BLESSINGS OF HOME

My safety harbour from the storm ~ My cozy haven safe and warm. No matter where I choose to roam...

...There's just no other place like home

D. Morgan

HARVEST HOUSE PUBLISHERS
EUGENE, OREGON 97402

BLESSINGS OF HOME

Copyright © 1998 Harvest House Publishers
Eugene, Oregon 97402

Library of Congress Cataloging-in-Publication Data
Morgan, D. (Doris)
      Blessings of home / D. Morgan.
          p.   cm.
      ISBN 1-56507-803-9
      1. Home--Quotations, maxims, etc.   I. Title.
      PN6084.H57M67   1998
      392.3--dc21   97-44462
                    CIP

D. Morgan's inspirational art and verse are featured in galleries and gift shops throughout the world.
She studied formally at The High Museum School of Art in Atlanta, Georgia, but credits her father
as her most influential teacher. Doris and her husband make their home in Georgia.

Artwork designs are reproduced under license from Arts Uniq', Inc., Cookeville, TN and may not be
reproduced without permission. For information regarding art prints featured in this book, please contact:

> Arts Uniq'
> P.O. Box 3085
> Cookeville TN 38502
> 1.800.223.5020

Harvest House Publishers has made every effort to trace the ownership of all poems and quotes.
In the event of a question arising from the use of any poem or quote, we regret any error made and
will be pleased to make the necessary correction in future editions of this book.

Scripture quotations are from The Living Bible, Copyright © 1971 owned by assignment by Illinois Regional Bank
N.A. (as trustee). Used by permission of Tyndale House Publishers, Inc., Wheaton, Illinois 60189. All rights reserved;
the Revised Standard Version of the Bible, Copyright 1946, 1952, 1971 by the Divison of Christian Education
of the National Council of Churches of Christ in the U.S.A. Used by permission.

Printed in the United States of America.

Design and production by
Koechel Peterson & Associates
Minneapolis, Minnesota

98 99 00 01 02 03 04 05 06 07 / WZ / 10 9 8 7 6 5 4 3 2 1

To my mother, Cornelia Slater Whitten,
who could always make a house feel like a home

To my daddy, John Lovic Whitten,
whose creative, imaginative heart and soul
have been indelibly imprinted on mine

To my print publishers, Barbara and Lonnie Crouch,
who came into my life at just the right time

To my licensing director, Jane Randolph,
whose undying belief in me, along with her unwavering
and persistent efforts, continues to guide me along paths
of new adventures and opportunities on which
I might have never traveled

and especially...

To my loving husband,
who is the "wind beneath my wings"

The little path that leads to home,
That is the road for me,
I know no finer path to roam,
With finer sights to see.

With thoroughfares the world is lined
That lead to wonders new,
But he who treads them leaves behind
The tender things and true.

Oh, north and south and east and west
The crowded roadways go,
And sweating brow and weary breast
Are all they seem to know.

And mad for pleasure some are bent,
And some are seeking fame,
And some are sick with discontent,
And some are bruised and lame.

Across the world the gleaming steel
Holds out its lure for men,
But no one finds his comfort real
Till he comes home again.

And charted lanes now line the sea
For weary hearts to roam,
But, oh, the finest path to me
Is that which leads to home.

'Tis there I come to laughing eyes
And find a welcome true;
'Tis there all care behind me lies
And joy is ever new.

And, oh, when every day is done
Upon that little street,
A pair of rosy youngsters run
To me with flying feet.

The world with myriad paths is lined
But one alone for me,
One little road where I may find
The charms I want to see.

Though thoroughfares majestic call
The multitude to roam,
I would not leave, to know them all,
The path that leads to home.

EDGAR A. GUEST

It gives me that pleasant ache just to think of coming to a really, truly home.

L.M. Montgomery ANNE OF GREEN GABLES

Home is the resort

Of love, of joy, of peace

and plenty, where,

Supporting and supported,

polish'd friends

And dear relations

mingle into bliss.

THOMSON

As shadows fall
The night birds call,
And I am home once more.
Safe from the storm
Where hearts are warm
The other side of....
....My Front Door.

I cherish all the memories

...Of every sight and sound

There among the gentle people...

D. Morgan 1985

Back in my home town.

The home we first knew on this beautiful earth,

The friends of our childhood,

the place of our birth,

In the heart's inner chamber sung always will be,

As the shell sings of its home in the sea.

FRANCES DANA GAGE
Home

Spread love everywhere you go: first of all in your own house.

Give love to your children, to your wife or husband, to a next door neighbor....

Let no one ever come to you without leaving better and happier.

Be the living expression of God's kindness; kindness in your face,

kindness in your eyes, kindness in your smile, kindness in your warm greeting.

MOTHER TERESA

Blest be that spot, where cheerful guests retire

To pause from toil, and trim their ev'ning fire;

Blest that abode, where want and pain repair,

And every stranger finds a ready chair.

GOLDSMITH

If I could do it all over again — and start my life anew...

.....Many a thing I'd do differently —

— But I'd do it again — with — you.

D. Morgan © 1993

*Sweet is
the smile of home;
the mutual look,
When hearts are of
each other sure.*

John Keeble

Peace, unto this house, I pray,

Keep terror and despair away;

Shield it from evil and let sin

Never find lodging room within.

May never in these walls be heard

The hateful or accusing word.

Grant that its warm and mellow light

May be to all a beacon bright,

A flaming symbol that shall stir

The beating pulse of him or her

Who finds this door and seems to say,

"Here ends the trials of the day."

EDGAR A. GUEST

His home, the spot of earth supremely blest, a dearer, sweeter spot than all the rest.

L. M. Montgomery

*H*is house was perfect,

whether you liked food, or sleep,

or work, or story-telling, or singing,

or just sitting and thinking best,

or a pleasant mixture of them all.

J.R.R. TOLKIEN
The Hobbit

I close my eyes and the memories of home rush to greet me. All the good times and hard times — the laughter and tears. For the rest of my life, no matter where I go, or what I do — My Favorite Place On Earth.... will always be ....Home.

D. Morgan © 1993

There were many pleasant houses on the wide, shady street. Magnolia, oak, and poplar trees grew all around our house. But the Chinaberry trees, with their limbs close to the ground, were best for climbing. The fragrance of honeysuckle was intoxicating.

On the small town square, birds fluttered amid the knobs and carvings of the old courthouse. Across the street, Tatum's drugstore soda fountain served a delicious concoction of lemon, lime, and lithia water.

It was a different world…when gentle people took time to enjoy the simple pleasures of gracious living.

D. MORGAN

But what on earth is half so dear—so longed for—as the hearth of home?

Emily Brontë A LITTLE WHILE

Dishes done
Papers read
Children snuggled into bed —
Hours past the setting sun —
I count my blessings ....
.... One By One.

D. Morgan ©1991

By the fireside, still the light is shining,

The children's arms round the parents twining.

From love so sweet, O who would roam?

Be it ever so homely, home is home.

D.M. MULOCK

Light shone in the windows of the bungalow.

Two square patches of gold fell upon the pinks and

the peaked marigolds. Florrie, the cat, came out on to the

verandah, and sat on the top of the step, her white paws

close together, her tail curled round. She looked content,

as though she had been waiting for this moment all day.

KATHERINE MANSFIELD
At the Bay

Winter is the time for comfort, for good food and warmth for the touch of a friendly hand and

beside the fire: it is the time for home.

Dame Edith Sitwell

for a talk

D. Morgan ©1988

My heart recalls

A childhood December—

A magical time,

So sweet

to

remember.

D. MORGAN

I remember the softness and charm of the wide shad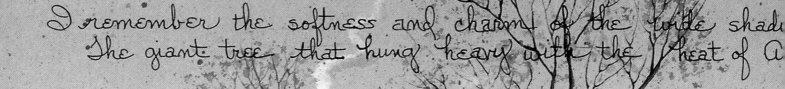
The giant tree that hung heavy with the heat of A

And in winter—
...the warm
contentm

D. Morgan © 1989

I love remembering the simple pleasures of my....

....Grandmother's

Ah, what is more blessed than to put cares away, when the mind lays by its burden, and tired with labour of far travel we have come to our own home and rest on the couch we have longed for? This it is which alone is worth all these toils.

CATULLUS

'Tis joy to him that toils, when toil is o'er,
To find a home waiting, full of happy things.

EURIPEDES

Peace and rest at length have come,
All the day's long toil is past;
And each heart is whispering, "Home, Home at last!"

THOMAS HOOD

There's a little
bit of heaven —
'round the corner take a right — a cozy little cottage with a little kitchen light...
...a comfort when I'm weary — a refuge when I'm blue —
There's a little bit of heaven here at home with you.

© 1988 D. Morgan

"*It* is but a cottage," she continued,

"but I hope to see many of my friends in it.

A room or two can easily be added;

and if my friends find no difficulty in travelling

so far to see me, I am sure I will find

none in accommodating them."

JANE AUSTEN
Sense and Sensibility

Cheerfully share your home with those who need a meal or a place to stay for the night.

The Book of 1 Peter

I will always remember
The special times that seemed so magical...

...At My Grandmothers' House.

D. Morgan© 1997

Home is the sphere

of harmony and peace,

The spot where angels find

a resting-place,

When, bearing blessings,

they descend to earth.

MRS. HALE

The happiness of the domestic fireside is the first boon of Heaven. . . .

Thomas Jefferson

God looks down well pleased to mark in earth's dusk each rosy spark.

Lights of home and lights of love, and the child the heart thereof.

Katherine Tynan, A NIGHT THOUGHT

Crosswicks was a house, a real house. We planted trees,

trees which would take an entire lifetime to mature.

The great elms in front of the house,

the bridal elms, had been planted as each

of the original daughters of the house was married.

Our trees, too, were an affirmation.

This was where we wanted to raise our family....

MADELEINE L'ENGLE
A Circle of Quiet

Through kitchen windows in the night,
When lamps are lit
And burning bright,
I feel that warm of long ago
From windows
I don't even know.

A light in a kitchen window
Finds me yesterday's best friend—
And sweetest memories surface
To
  Take
    Me
      Home
        Again.

D. MORGAN

In happy homes he saw the light

Of household fires gleam warm and bright.

Henry Wadsworth Longfellow

No place on earth I'ee ever find —

...... Like home — so gentle on my mind.

D. Morgan © 1987

Sweet are the joys of home, and pure as sweet; for they,

Like dews of morn and evening, come to wake and close the day.

The world hath its delights, and its delusions, too;

But home to calmer bliss invites, more tranquil and more true.

John Bowring

And when

Let us guide our children with wisdom ~
Let us listen to their problems
And help them find solutions.
Let us give them
Unconditional
Love ~
No
Matter
What ......

they are grown,
let us find the courage to let go.

D. Morgan © 1990

It is beautiful, my house. It is bare, of course, but the wind, the sun, the smell of the pines blow

I love my seashell of a house. I wish I could live in it always.

Anne Morrow Lindbergh GIFT FROM THE SEA

D. Morgan © 1990

"How the home lights shine out through the dark!" said Anne.

"That string of them over the harbor looks like a necklace.

And what a coruscation there is up at the Glen!

Oh, look, Gilbert, there is ours. I'm so glad we left it burning.

I hate to come home to a dark house.

Our homelight, Gilbert! Isn't it lovely to see?"

L. M. MONTGOMERY
Anne's House of Dreams

If solid happiness we prize,

Within our breast this jewel lies,

And they are fools who roam.

The world has nothing to bestow;

From our own selves our joys must flow,

And that dear hut, our home.

NATHANIEL COLTON
The Fireside

D. Morgan © 1985

Coming home, there is no corner of my mind unoccupied with memories.

What a lovely time it was.

I can see Daddy, with arms full of new puppies,

and hear Mother singing in the kitchen.

And for one fleeting moment, I am home, a child again.

D. MORGAN

No place is more delightful than one's own fireside.

Cicero

D. Morgan © 1989

Home may be near,

Home may be far—

But it is anywhere love

And a few plain household treasures are.

GRACE NOLL CROWELL

Radio, sewing machine, book ends, ironing board and that great big piano lamp—peace, that's what I like.

I hear your footsteps on the pathway, the turn of your

I find my fears are unfounded — you are safe

key in the door ~

...and home once more.   D. Morgan © 1993

His warm

but simple home

where he enjoys

With her who shares his

pleasure and his heart,

Sweet converse.

COWPER

*P*eace be to you, and peace be to your house,

and peace be to all that you have.

THE BOOK OF 1 SAMUEL

*A*s much as I converse with sages and heroes,

they have very little of my love and admiration.

I long for rural and domestic scenes, for the warbling

of birds and the prattling of my children.

JOHN ADAMS
Letter to His Wife, 16 March, 1777

Our family forms a circle, where thoughts of love are spoken. Through life's good times and hard times, too, our love remains unbroken.

WELCOME

D. Morgan © 1996

God send us a little home,

To come back to, when we roam.

Low walls and fluted tiles,

Wide windows, a view for miles.

Red firelight and deep chairs,

Small white bed upstairs—

Great talk in little nooks,

Dim colors, rows of books.

One picture on each wall,

Not many things at all.

God send us a little ground,

Tall trees stand round.

Homely flowers in brown sod,

Overhead, thy stars, O God.

God bless them, when winds blow,

Our home and all we know.

FLORENCE BONE